The Coming JOB BOOM

The Coming JOB BOOM

✦

Why the Employment Market for Young Graduates Has Never Been Better

Dr. Ira Wolfe
Dr. Bonnie Snyder

iUniverse, Inc.
New York Lincoln Shanghai

The Coming JOB BOOM
Why the Employment Market for Young Graduates Has Never Been Better

iUniverse books may be ordered through booksellers or by contacting:

iUniverse
2021 Pine Lake Road, Suite 100
Lincoln, NE 68512
www.iuniverse.com
1-800-Authors (1-800-288-4677)

Because of the dynamic nature of the Internet, any Web addresses or links contained in this book may have changed since publication and may no longer be valid.

ISBN: 978-0-595-48316-7 (pbk)
ISBN: 978-0-595-60404-3 (ebk)

Printed in the United States of America

Published and Distributed by Poised for the Future Company Lancaster, Pennsylvania USA

Cover photography by Getty Images. Used by permission.

This book is dedicated to the new generation of graduates.

May all your career dreams come true.

"There is a tide in the affairs of men,

Which, taken at the flood, leads on to fortune;

Omitted, all the voyage of their life

Is bound in shallows and in miseries."

—William Shakespeare
Julius Caesar Act IV, Scene iii

Contents

The Future's So Bright ...

Back in the 1980s, the band Timbuk 3 had a big hit with the song, "The Future's So Bright I Gotta Wear Shades." The lyrics started out like so:

> I study nuclear science, I love my classes
> I got a crazy teacher, he wears dark glasses
> Things are going great, and they're only getting better
> I'm doin' all right, getting good grades
> The future's so bright I gotta wear shades

It's a catchy song and in the early eighties it did seem for a while like the future was going to be incredibly bright. Unfortunately, the employment reality for young graduates at that time didn't turn out to be quite so rosy. Young adults entering the workforce during the late eighties graduated smack into a major economic recession. To make matters much worse, they were entering a workforce already filled to overflowing with older, more experienced employees from the largest generation in American history—the Baby Boomers—who *themselves* were being downsized. Oh, and there was a major stock market crash to boot. So much for needing sunglasses!

High school and even college graduates during those years took whatever jobs they could get and counted themselves lucky. Many found themselves underemployed, working at jobs well below their capabilities—so-called "McJobs." In fact, this predicament was the original premise of the show "Friends." (Remember the opening theme song? "Well no one told you life was gonna be this way. You're job's a joke, you're broke …") Those graduates eventually found jobs, but when they looked up the ladder of advancement, they saw what has been called the "gray ceiling;" their path of advancement was blocked by older boomers who would be in the workworld in senior positions for a long, long time.

... *You're Gonna Need Shades*

That was then, this is now. If you're lucky enough to be a young graduate or soon-to-be graduate reading this book, it looks like you were born at the right time. (Not that you can take any credit for it.) The employment picture is shaping up to be very bright, indeed. Demographic forces are aligning to create what looks to be the best seller's job market in the last century. You see, the Baby Boomers are aging and the oldest ones will begin retiring around the year 2010. The demand for young, educated workers is already heating up and all signs point to a future of unlimited possibilities for those who are ambitious and well-prepared. Instead of looking up at the "gray ceiling," *your* career forecast is calling for nothing but sunny skies for the foreseeable future. Congratulations.

There is an old saying that, "Chance favors the well-prepared." In other words, to make the most of your potential opportunities in this future seller's job market, you need to have a clear view of what is coming and the forces that are at work. The outlook is brighter in some fields than in others, and the workplace is changing. You want to be sure that you are changing with it, and preparing yourself to advance as quickly as possible.

Because there are more aging, soon-to-be-retiring Baby Boomers than young workers to replace them, labor shortages are predicted for at least the next *ten to twenty years*. Another emerging problem is that a lot of older workers don't have the necessary technology skills to handle today's jobs. Wages are already exploding for skilled workers and for any job whose demand is outstripping supply.

The employment road ahead is filled with opportunity for those who have the foresight to see what is coming, so grab your shades as we take a look at the sunny employment outlook and the forces affecting it in more detail in the pages ahead.

More Jobs for Graduates

Year to year, the economy may be good or the economy may be bad, but remember this: demography is destiny! Huge, statistical forces are far more powerful than mere economic ones. As the enormous baby-boomer generation retires from the workforce over the next 10-20 years, employers will be clamoring for replacements and competing with one another to hire them. That's great news for you.

The coming workforce changes are an inevitable part of the greatest demographic change in human history. As 76 million Baby Boomers reach retirement age, the younger age group directly behind them is significantly smaller—about 16 percent fewer in number, according to reports published in the *Atlanta Business Chronicle*.

The fact of the matter is that Americans have been having fewer children and living longer lives for the past several decades. The result is that what used to be a demographic pyramid, with a small number of elderly at the top and a wide base of many children at the bottom, has turned into a column, or "silo", with its mid-portion—the primary workforce—shrinking. Because of the "baby bust" and "birth dearth" of the 1970s and early 80s, when Boomers chose to have smaller families, we are moving into a period of declining work-aged citizens. Generation X, which came right after the Boomers, is nearly half their size at only 46 million.

Statistical charts depict the dramatic shift in our national demographics which is soon going to be emptying our national workforce. At the turn of the last century (1900), demographic charts showed very few older people and a lot of younger people. The charts ended up looking like a pyramid, because each older age group was naturally a little smaller than the younger age group below it, due to deaths. Well, that's not what's happening anymore. These days, our demographic chart has turned into more of a rectangle, since the older generations are living longer and people are not having as many children. In fact, there's actually an indentation in the middle, right after the Baby Boomers, which means there are more older people than younger people. (To see what this looks like in graphic form, visit **www.comingjobboom.com**.)

The American workforce is also aging. The median age of the labor force in 2010 will rise to its highest level since 1962, almost 41 years. The Baby Boomers are already entering their sixties. The oldest of the vast Baby Boomer generation are set to reach their 65th year—traditional retirement age—in the year 2011. Every older person who retires from the workforce creates a need for a younger person to step into that position. The young graduate who is ambitious, educated, and prepared for the workworld will find a ready reception.

During the coming decades, there are going to be more older people than younger, working-aged people, which is unprecedented in human history! This is the source of the Coming JOB BOOM. The bottom line is that jobs will continue to be plentiful for years to come, but workers will not. And that presents a tremendous opportunity for young people with the skills and attitudes required by these soon-to-be desperate employers.

The facts are irrefutable. In 2006, the first of the Boomers hit 60 and became eligible for pensions. In 2008, Boomers will reach 62 and can begin drawing early Social Security benefits, and in 2011 they will reach age 65.

At that point, the number of people in the United States celebrating their 65th birthday will jump 22 percent, from 2.7 million to 3.3 million.[1] According to Harris Interactive,

> The number of retiring 'Boomers' will continue to grow steadily until 2030, when one U.S. resident in five will be over 65, compared to one in eight now. What was a nagging concern just a few years ago has become a major issue with over 80% of employers expressing concern and almost 30% feeling very or extremely concerned.[2]

Employers worldwide are already struggling to find and retain qualified workers. A combination of aging population demographics, a growing economy, and fewer qualified workers to fill the void are making labor a scarce commodity. In other words, in a labor shortage, it's a seller's market for job hunters!

Future labor shortages are here to stay and will begin to hit full force around the end of this decade, by 2010. The statistics are stunning. Starting in 2012, nearly 10,000 Americans will turn 65 every day. The number of workers age 55 and over is growing four times faster than the workforce as a whole. Baby Boomers, who in 2006 ranged in age from 42 to 60, currently represent one-half of the U.S. workforce. This is slightly more than the number of workers from the succeeding two generations, Generation X and the Millennial Generation (Generation Y) *combined*. In contrast, the number of workers ages 35-44 is projected to *decrease* by 10%. The segment of the population that is 65 and older will grow by more than 80% during the same time period. According to *Time* Magazine,

As the population ages, hospitals can't find enough nurses or medical technicians. Drugstores are competing to hire pharmacists, bidding some beginners' salaries above $75,000. School districts and universities will need 2.2 million more teachers over the next decade, not to mention administrators and librarians, and are already avidly recruiting. Homeowners can't get their calls returned by skilled contractors, electricians or plumbers. Corporations are scooping up accountants and engineers. For job seekers who have the right skills or are willing to learn them, there are real opportunities in government, construction and technology.[3]

In 1980, the United States had over seven million more people available to work than there were jobs available. The unemployment rate was 7.1 percent. By 2000, there were four million more jobs available than people to work them, and the unemployment rate was a mere 4%. Bureau of Labor Statistics (BLS) data forecast a shortage of *more than 10 million workers* by the year 2010. That's just around the corner.

Job seekers can expect to see less competition for job openings through at least 2050. The anticipated result will be higher salaries, more training and career advancement opportunities, and more flexible work cultures—great news for the new entrant to the workforce.

It all spells O-P-P-O-R-T-U-N-I-T-Y for you.

Increasing Demand for Educated Workers

The employment outlook may be good, but that doesn't mean that you don't have to prepare yourself for the coming opportunities. No matter how good the job market is, the bar has been raised: if you want a good job with a competitive salary and an opportunity to grow and advance, you will need more and better skills. If you lack the necessary skills to do a worthwhile job, no one is going to want to hire you. If, by chance, you *are* hired in spite of poor preparation, the likelihood of job satisfaction is small and the chance of frustration high.

On the other hand, if you enter the job market prepared to meet a potential employers' needs, you may well find yourself in the enviable position of having several employers competing for *you*.

Businesses today don't just need bodies to fill the available positions; they need skilled and educated workers, able to handle challenging tasks. In 2030, as 77 million baby boomers leave the workforce, there will be twice as many retirees as there are today, but only 18 percent more workers. According to some leading estimates, by 2008 the U.S. economy will offer nearly 161 million jobs to 155 million workers. The Hudson Institute predicts that the supply of skilled labor in the United States will not catch up to demand until the year 2050.[4]

Many employers are finding that potential new employees are sorely lacking in required educational competencies. This is causing increasing demand for well-educated workers. Basic literacy and numeracy skills are also a growing problem among recent graduates of both high schools *and* colleges.

Couple that with rising dropout rates—currently, about 1.3 million students drop out of high school each year—to appreciate the magnitude of the problem. The number of dropouts has grown over the past thirty years; according to the National Center for Education Statistics, the population segment of American 16-24-year-olds who were not enrolled in school or who did not have a high school diploma or a GED credential was about 11 percent in 2001.

Global forces are also exerting pressures on U.S. firms and changing the nature of American jobs. Routine work is increasingly done by machines and by lower-paid people in less-developed countries. Intense competition from these overseas workers, willing to work for lower pay, means that many high-paying, low skill American jobs are a thing of the past. This growing competition is forcing American employers to require different skill sets and character qualities from the people they hire.

As a result, jobs in the United States are moving towards more complex and innovative work, including research, development, design, and marketing and sales.[5] Americans can no longer compete in the world markets based on price only, because the rest of the world is willing to work for less than we are. We have no choice but to compete based on our level of ingenuity and innovation. These job requirements mean that American workers will need to be better educated with more advanced skills than ever before to compete effectively in the future.

Author Ira Wolfe, in his consulting practice, tells employers that they need to PICK the right employees. PICK represents Pace, Innovation, Complexity and Knowledge/Skills. Thanks to technology, the **pace** of change is happening faster. To be competitive, employers are continuously looking for ways to do more with less. That means workers will need to work smarter and faster through **innovation**. Employees who can keep up with the pace of work and pace of change will be the hot prospects.

In addition to innovation, the **complexity** of work is increasing. Often times, the pace of change and rate of innovation alone make even routine work more complex. Sometimes, work needs to be completed before all the answers are available. Job opportunities will abound for employees who can innovate quickly in ambiguous situations. Finally, complexity means that **knowledge** and skills will be the fuel that drives performance. Those candidates with the know-how will control the keys to their destiny.

To compete economically on a global scale, experts insist that American firms have to focus on creating products and services with high added value.[6] This requires an educated workforce. Unfortunately, the United States is falling behind on the world stage. Even some of the lower-paid countries, like India and China, are surpassing us in terms of education.

The fact is, although the United States had the best-educated workforce in the world for most of the 20th century, that is no longer true. According to the National Center on Education and the Economy, Americans have been losing ground educationally for the past 30 years, as one country after another has surpassed us in terms of the proportion of their workforce with a high school diploma or its equivalent. The NCEE states, "Thirty years ago, the United States could lay claim to having 30 percent of the world's population of college students. Today that proportion has fallen to 14 percent and is continuing to fall"[7]

Therefore, it stands to reason that *highly educated* young American workers are going to be exceptionally prized for two main reasons: the demographic squeeze caused by retiring Baby Boomers *and* the competitiveness squeeze caused by increased global competition. Poorly educated workers with few skills run the risk of being left behind.

What Employers Want

Future American economic might is going to depend on our ability to maintain our worldwide technological lead. We will have to create, and continue to create, breakthrough innovative technologies. According to a report entitled *Tough Choices or Tough Times: The Report of the New Commission on the Skills of the American Workforce*, "that kind of leadership does not depend on technology alone. It depends on a deep vein of creativity that is constantly renewing itself, and on a myriad of people who can imagine how people can use things that have never been available before, create ingenious marketing and sales campaigns, write books, build furniture, make movies, and imagine new kinds of software that will capture people's imagination."[8] The authors of this report assert that,

> A very high level of preparation in reading, writing, speaking, mathematics, science, literature, history, and the arts will be an indispensable foundation for everything that comes after for most members of the workforce. It is a world in which comfort with ideas and abstractions is the passport to a good job, in which creativity and innovation are the key to the good life, in which high levels of education—a very different kind of education than most of us have had—are going to be the only security there is.[9]

Consider the following employer outlooks from a different report entitled, *Are They Really Ready to Work? Employers' Perspectives on the Basic Knowledge and Applied Skills of New Entrants to the 21st Century U.S. Workforce* which was prepared by The Conference Board. After surveying corporate representative and senior executives about their expectations for new hires, the report concludes that young workers are most deficient in the following areas: *Oral and Written Communications, Professionalism/Work Ethic, and Critical Thinking/Problem Solving*. This is particularly true of students who have never attended college, but the findings indicate that even college graduates have deficiencies that make it hard for willing employers to hire them. For example, employers report than one-quarter of four-year college graduates lack basic ability with Written Communications.[10]

Employers also state that they expect new employees to have a sense of Professionalism and a strong Work Ethic, but that too often new hires lack these important qualities. Professionalism includes factors such as dressing properly, showing up on time, meeting commitments, and behaving maturely. "We have experienced horrendous turnover rates among high school graduates we hire," says one corporate representative. "We hire these young people, and then they don't come to work. And they don't see a problem with being absent. And when they do come, what they seem to care about is when they can leave work."[11]

When ranking the skill levels of recent hires in a report card format, new graduates were found to be "Adequate" or "Deficient" far more often than "Excellent." Written communication is a particularly large problem, particularly for high school graduates, since 80.9 percent of employers rated them "deficient" in this skill. An inability to handle basic writing skills such as using correct grammar and spelling is the most frequently noted problem in young workers' basic knowledge. In fact, Written Communication is the most frequently reported problem with hires for *all* educational levels, including college graduates. Specific problems with writing skills and ineffective business communication skills include spelling errors, improper use of grammar, and the misuse of words in written reports, PowerPoint presentations, and email messages.[12] The ease of electronic communication (and the decreased use of formal business letters) may be contributing to a very casual approach to the proper use of the English language among younger generations.

The employers in this study then listed their expectations (in order of importance) for potential new hires at three different educational levels, including a "report card" on their current level of preparation. The following information gives you a clear picture of exactly which key skills employers are looking for:

EMPLOYERS' REPORT CARD ON WORKFORCE READINESS

High School Graduates

The following ten workplace skills were considered very important for high school graduates to possess (in order):

1. Professionalism/Work Ethic (80.3% indicated very important)

2. Teamwork/Collaboration (74.7%)

3. Oral Communications (70.3%)

4. Ethics/Social Responsibility (63.4%)

5. Reading Comprehension (62.5%)

6. English Language (61.8%)

7. Critical Thinking/Problem Solving (57.5%)

8. Information Technology (53.0%)

9. Written Communications (52.7%)

10. Diversity (52.1%)

Unfortunately, high school graduates overall were perceived by employers as being deficient or below expectations in all the major areas considered important. As you can see, a very high percentage (80.9%) indicated that Written Communications was the most deficient skill, followed closely by Professionalism/Work Ethic.

Skills Appraisal

BELOW EXPECTATIONS

Written communications (80.9%)

Professionalism/Work Ethic (70.3%)

Critical Thinking/Problem Solving (69.6%)

Oral Communications (52.7%)

Ethics/Social Responsibility (44.1%)

Reading Comprehension (38.4%)

Teamwork/Collaboration (34.6%)

Diversity (27.9%)

Information Technology Application (21.5%)

English Language (21.0%)

EXCELLENT

Unfortunately, no skills were on the "Excellent" list for high school graduates.

Two-Year College/Technical School Graduates

The following skills were ranked as most important for two-year graduates to possess:

1. Professionalism/Work Ethic (83.4% very important)

2. Teamwork/Collaboration (82.7%)

3. Oral Communications (82.0%)

4. Critical thinking/Problem Solving (72.7%)

5. Reading Comprehension (71.6%)

6. Written Communications (71.5%)

7. English Language (70.6%)

8. Ethics/Social Responsibility (70.6%)

9. Information Technology (68.6%)

10. Writing in English (64.9%)

While the expected skills for two-year graduates are similar to the expectations for high school graduates, fewer skills were rated as being "Deficient" or "Below Expectations" at this educational level, and two-year graduates' applied information technology skills were ranked as "Excellent." Even though written communications is still perceived to be the number one deficient skill, the number of employers' indicating this is a problem drops considerably at this level.

Skills Appraisal

BELOW EXPECTATIONS

Written Communications (47.3%)

Writing in English (46.4%)

Lifelong Learning/Self Direction (27.9%)

Creativity/Innovation (27.6%)

Critical Thinking/Problem Solving (22.8%)

Oral Communications (21.3%)

Ethics/Social Responsibility (21.0%)

EXCELLENT

Applied Information Technology

Four-Year College Graduates

The list of skills desired of college graduates is longer than the lists for high school or two-year graduates, indicating higher expectations for this elite group.

1. Oral Communications (95.4% very important)

2. Teamwork/Collaboration (94.4%)

3. Professionalism/Work Ethic (93.8%)

4. Written Communications (93.1%)

5. Critical Thinking/Problem Solving (92.1%)

6. Writing in English (89.7%)

7. English Language (88.0%)

8. Reading Comprehension (87.0%)

9. Ethics/Social Responsibility (85.6%)

10. Leadership (81.8%)

11. Information Technology (81.0%)

12. Creativity/Innovation (81.0%)

13. Lifelong Learning/Self Direction (78.3%)

14. Diversity (71.8%)

15. Technology (81%)

16. Creativity/Innovation (81.0%)

17. Lifelong Learning/Self Direction (78.3%)

18. Diversity (71.8%)

It appears that the extra years of education for a college degree are paying off, since the list of skills rated "excellent" by employers includes nine items, and there are only three skills listed as being deficient or below expectations. Most notable among them is written communications.

Skills Appraisal

BELOW EXPECTATIONS

Written Communications (27.8%)

Writing in English (26.2%)

Leadership (23.8%)

EXCELLENT

Applied Information Technology
Diversity
Critical Thinking/Problem Solving
English Language
Lifelong learning/Self direction
Reading Comprehension
Oral Communication
Teamwork/Collaboration
Creativity/Innovation[13]

Not surprisingly, college graduates also earn more. Recent census figures indicate that a college degree is worth about $23,000 extra each year, compared to having only a high school diploma. College graduates made an average of $51,554 in 2004, compared with $28,645 for adults with a high school diploma. High school dropouts earned an average of $19,169 and those with advanced college degrees made an average of $78,093.

Overall, the authors of the Conference Board employer report conclude that, "the best employers the world over will be looking for the most competent, most creative, and most innovative people on the face of the earth and will be willing to pay them top dollar for their services … Strong skills in English, mathematics, technology, and science, as well as literature, history, and the arts will be essential for many; beyond this, candidates will have to be comfortable with ideas and abstractions, good at both analysis and synthesis, creative and innovative, self-disciplined and well organized, able to learn very quickly and work well as a member of a team."[14] To access the best of what the future has to offer, these are the skills young workers are going to have to develop.

Finding the Right Job for You

It's undoubtedly comforting to know that you can expect there to be plentiful jobs for new graduates during the coming years, but the truth is, you only need *one* job. How do you find the job that's right for you?

First off, you want to begin with self-knowledge. You need to be aware of your own interests, strengths, personal values, and motivation to ensure that you find a job that will not just pay you enough money, but that will be satisfying in other ways, as well. If you find yourself in a job that makes you unhappy, you are unlikely to perform well. This can lead to frustration, poor references, and lost advancement opportunities.

Your high school guidance office and college career counseling center offer assessments to help students identify their key interests, values, and strengths. You will certainly want to take advantage of all the services offered through your school. If you would like to receive professional testing services to help you determine your career strengths and appropriate job clusters, you may want to contact Success Performance Solutions to learn about our testing products and how they can help you gain the self-knowledge necessary to make good choices. You can learn more about the benefits of career testing by visiting **www.super-solutions.com.**

Get Ready for Opportunity

Now is the time to make plans for a great career. The job market may be good, but that doesn't mean you don't need to prepare for success. Thanks to demographic shifts, there is every reason for you to be optimistic about your employment prospects, but you also need to take responsibility for developing the work ethic and professional demeanor that will have employers clamoring to hire *you*. The young person who approaches the coming workforce opportunities with a clear sense of purpose and drive will find a warm reception and swift advancement in the workforce and be off to a great start. The greatest career successes are very clear about what it is they want as they enter the workforce.

So, begin by asking yourself:

What kind of job am I trying to find?
What type of employer am I hoping to attract?

Until you can answer these very basic questions, your career is stalled. You are liable to jump at the very first offer you receive, and you could land in the wrong position. If you wind up in a job that's not appropriate for you, you could quickly become unmotivated, unhappy, and low-performing. If you are unsuccessful in your first position and need to look elsewhere, you may be forced to leave without a good recommendation for your next job. This can really hold you back. That's why it's important to get it right the first time.

It is valuable to consider your personal strengths realistically and then match these to the present job opportunities. The Roman philosopher Seneca said that "luck is what happens when preparation meets opportunity." You create your own luck by first engaging in adequate preparation and then applying this to the opportunities you encounter.

Professional Behavior

To achieve all that you are capable of achieving and to succeed in the adult workforce, you will have to develop a sense of professionalism. This includes every aspect of how you communicate and how you present yourself, including your dress and behavior.

Having a solid educational background is only the start to career success. Like it or not, potential employers are also going to form opinions about you based on how you dress, behave, speak, and carry yourself. When you present a polished professional image, their opinions are likely to be favorable and your career advancement will be enhanced. If you present an unprofessional image, it is like you are telling your superiors that you are not really serious about your career and that you should not be considered for higher levels of responsibility. Don't let this happen to you. You could give this impression by dressing too casually for the job, failing to follow appropriate business etiquette, and producing shoddy or inferior work.

Your Appearance

Like it or not, in the workworld you are going to be judged, at least partly, by your appearance. If your clothes don't convey a professional image, you are sending the message that you may not be able to handle your job. Whether or not that's accurate, this *perception* of your ability is very important.

Model your work wardrobe on your supervisors and those around you. Consider the age-old advice: "dress for the job you want, not the job you have." Supervisors and decision-makers may have trouble picturing you in a higher role if you don't already dress the part. When in doubt, overdress for any work occasion. Of course, personal grooming is also an important part of your overall appearance. As always, take your cues from those in jobs above yours. Dress codes vary considerably between different fields, so make sure that you are dressing correctly for your job.

Workplace Behavior

If you are unsure about what is appropriate and acceptable in the workplace, you should ask your supervisor. It's also a good idea to invest in a book on basic etiquette before entering the professional world. Behavior that is tolerated in school or in college may not be acceptable at work. Some ways to convey an unprofessional image are showing up late, taking long lunches, or leaving early. Other ways to behave unprofessionally include sending or forwarding emails unrelated to work, making inappropriate jokes, poor hygiene, gossiping, flirting with coworkers, fooling around on the job, and talking too much about your personal life while at work. Banish these immature habits before you take your first job, or you could be hampered by a bad reputation that can stick with you for years.

Generally speaking, if you exhibit basic manners and focus on business matters when at work, you will convey a professional image. Also, clearly, how well you do your job will play a very important role in your professional image. Producing low quality work, handing in late reports, failing to check facts and details—these can all harm your career. In short, your professional image is everything you do and say in the workplace, including how you look. It is about producing quality work *and* presenting yourself as a quality individual. It can be a difficult transition from the casual atmosphere of the classroom to the more refined workworld, but it is important that you make the effort. When you pull all of these elements of professionalism together into a mature, polished, business-like package, you will be perceived as an equal and taken seriously. You will also be a serious contender when retirements inevitably occur and promotions become available!

Gather references as you go

In the business world, employers like to "check your references." These are a lot like the letters of recommendations applicants gather from their high school teachers before applying to college. So, as you prepare to graduate and enter the workworld, look around and ask yourself who would be willing to recommend you enthusiastically to potential employers. In fact, it's wise to think of all the people you interact with as "potential references" and to treat them in such a way that you would be proud to have any one of them write a recommendation letter on your behalf.

Never leave one job or school program and move onto another without asking for suitable references from those you are leaving behind. In fact, it's better not to leave anyone "behind," but to maintain your contacts as much as possible. These days, with the help of the internet and social networking sites, staying connected is easier than ever. So, if you are entering your final quarter of high school or your last semester of college, now is the time to ask for those all-important job references from people who admire you and your work. Once you have switched locations, it is much harder to collect them.

Take control of your career path

Whether you work for a small company or for a large corporation, you are still in charge of your own career. Think of yourself as being in business yourself and remember that you're the boss of "YOU Corporation." You and only you are responsible for the success of your career, and no one will care as much about your career path as you do.

You should develop your own strategic plan for your life and for your career—the same as any business should plan for the future. You must set your own goals and hold yourself accountable for meeting them. Again, don't expect your boss or manager to do this for you. Take responsibility for achieving the goals that are important to you by spelling them out clearly at the outset of your career.

Many career coaches these days recommend that you "brand" yourself in the workforce. "Branding" simply means positioning yourself in order to get noticed. Think of different brands of products you might see in the store. They all seek to be a little bit different from each other by promoting whatever it is that makes each of them distinct and sets them apart.

Your brand is what you are known for—your reputation. What do you want to be known for? What is it that sets you apart from the rest of the crowd and distinguishes you from other applicants? If you were a manager responsible for hiring people to an organization, would you hire you? It is important to consider the answers to these questions, because they can help to guide you in creating your personal career identity and crafting a compelling resume. The better you know and understand yourself, the better you will be able to convince others of the specific benefits you offer and why they should want you as part of their team.

Your resume is one important tool for branding yourself, but these days, it's not enough. Employers are also apt to research your "online identity" and, according to *Business Week* (June 26, 2006) about 35% of executive recruiters have eliminated potential job candidates based on what they found out about them online.

So, go ahead and Google your name right now and see what comes up. Googling yourself is the modern equivalent of the traditional "reference check." If you have left behind an unprofessional trail of blog entries and Facebook postings, you need to take the time to remove these before applying for positions! Otherwise, they could come back to haunt you.

On the other hand, if you are "anonymous" or nonexistent online, this can send the message that you are technologically behind the times. You want to make it easy for employers not only to find you online, but to find what you want them to see.

One of the best ways to do this is to construct your own website.

This can a tremendous self-promotion tool. You can mention any awards that you've won and exhibit a professional portfolio online, since you control all the content. You can also link to any other sites on which you have a positive presence. You may also want to join clubs related to your career goals and then make sure that your name is included in their webpages. Ideally, your online presence will be linked with positive organizations related to your career which will help to reinforce your personal career "brand."

Be selective

Even in the best of circumstances, a job hunt can be a stressful experience. When you go to an interview, you worry about making a good impression and getting the interviewer to like you. You try to answer the questions the "right" way. You're probably focusing on convincing them to hire you. That's all good, but you also need to remember that *you* are hiring your new boss—the person who will have the power to set you on the fast track or on the wrong track, altogether. That's why you need to remember what your long-term goals are and be selective about the positions you are willing to seriously consider accepting.

Remember: an interview is always a two-way process. They are meeting you *and* you are meeting them. They may be asking you a lot of questions, but don't forget to interview them! Don't be so concerned with impressing *them* that you forget to ask your own questions or to find out whether you like the organization enough to even consider working there. Hopefully, with the coming labor shortages, you will be able to be fairly selective about the job you choose.

You need to know what you are getting into before you accept your first job offer. If you don't think that you will get along with your potential new boss, think twice before taking the position. It may be smarter to pass on this opportunity and wait for something more appropriate for you.

You want to find a boss who is interested in you, your career, and your development. The ideal boss can even serve as a coach and a mentor to you, helping you to achieve your own career goals in alignment with the goals of the organization. When you find a good boss and you get along well, you improve your chances for advancement tremendously. If your boss is also a rising star within the organization, so much the better for you!

Your potential employer is going to be doing a background check on you, so you should check out their references, as well. Before accepting a position, look into the organization's, and the boss's reputation. How long have other employees stayed with this employer? What is the turnover rate? A high turnover rate should be a warning sign that employees do not find working with this manager or organization satisfying over the long term. If they can't retain employees, there must be a reason why.

When you have a good relationship with your boss, you can advance very, very rapidly. One of the best ways to develop a solid relationship with your boss is to try to make him or her look good whenever you can. This works in your own favor, because good bosses like employees who make them look good. When you help your boss to advance, you should advance along with him or her.

To build a strong, positive relationship with your boss, it helps to recognize and anticipate your boss's needs and help meet them. Your boss has projects to complete and important goals and objectives to accomplish. Find out what they are, and then ask yourself what you can contribute to help your boss achieve them. Your assistance in helping your boss to accomplish key priorities will be appreciated and, if you have chosen a good boss, rewarded. And, at work, always keep your commitments and meet your deadlines, since your boss is counting on you.

Working well with other generations

To succeed in the future workplace, you're going to have to learn how to get along with people of different ages. That's because the workworld has become increasingly "age diverse."

As the "new kid" on the block, you are going to have to get along with the older generations on the job. You will want to demonstrate respect for their hard-earned experience. Remember that senior level employees don't want to be shown up by a young hotshot, no matter how smart or savvy you are. So, even though you may have impressive academic credentials and advanced technological skills, you must be use tact and learn to get along with employees of different ages who may have different strengths.

Each generation in the workplace is different, with distinctive traits and values shaped by the era in which they were raised. Because members of the same generation have the same basic set of formative experiences, they tend to share certain assumptions in common. Understanding those different assumptions can help you to enjoy better relationships with others on the job.

Right now, there are four distinct generations occupying the workplace: the Traditional Generation, Baby Boomers, Generation X, and Generation Y. The older generations have traditionally viewed the younger generation with a certain amount of skepticism, complaining about their poor work ethic, so be prepared for this as a new young employee.

Each generation has its own particular identity. The Traditional Generation grew up during World War II and many of them served in the military; they believe strongly in values like sacrifice and patriotism. They like it when the workworld is structured like the military, with clear ranks and hierarchies. This generation tended to stay in one town or with one employer for an entire lifetime and career. These workers now comprise a small minority of the workforce and they will all be retired soon.

When the Baby Boomers first entered the workforce, they had to follow the rules established by their managers from the Traditional generation in order to succeed. So, Boomers tend to have a lot in common with the Traditionals. Because Boomers, by virtue of their numbers, also had more competition than any other generation, they learned to put in long hours to "get ahead" of their peers. Boomers, by and large, are known for putting their work ahead of their personal lives and they expected to be rewarded for their sacrifices the way the older generation had been. Instead, many Boomers were downsized in middle age during the economic recessions of the late 1980s, and they learned the hard way that lifetime loyalty to an employer is not always rewarded.

This was around the same time that Generation X entered the workworld. This generation is much smaller than the Boomers, born during the "Baby Bust" years between 1965 and 1977. Many members of Generation X had a neglected, "latchkey" childhood while their Boomer parents put in long hours at work, climbing the corporate ladder. Following the Boomers, members of Generation X quickly recognized that their career progress was going to be stalled for decades by the "grey ceiling" of older workers ahead of them. They had also already seen that loyalty to an employer doesn't necessarily pay off, by observing the way the workforce treated their parents.

In response, they demanded work-life balance and many chose to start their own businesses in response to limited traditional job opportunities. Because of this, some members of the older generation labeled them "slackers" unwilling to "pay their dues." Gen Xers eagerly seized upon the computer revolution, however, and quickly learned the new technology. Members of this generation were the original computer nerd "wunderkinds," and helped to create the internet. Their technical savvy meant that, for the first time ever, the younger employees in the workforce had to teach the older employees how to handle technology at work. Their impressive technological skills have ultimately made Gen Xers highly valued employees and able entrepreneurs.

The youngest generation in the workforce is Generation Y (right after X)—sometimes called the Millennials. Gen Y shares many of the same traits as Gen X, but to an even greater degree. One of the main factors setting this genera-tion apart is the extremely high level of technological sophistication it possesses. Y is the first generation that *always* had a computer. Y is also more global and sophisticated than previous generations. Observers say they also have higher expectations, because they have grown up with indulgent, nurturing parents and "instant" everything. They are accustomed to staying in touch constantly through cellphones. Unlike older generations which coveted conformity, this generation expects to personalize everything and to share their opinions on every subject on blogs, MySpace accounts, and on websites. Some believe that Gen Y's social skills are lacking, due to too much independent "screen time" during childhood.

Some employers worry that younger employees will turn out to be job-hoppers, so they may be hesitant to trust you with important assignments or to rely on you. The fact is that younger employees do tend to switch jobs much more often than older employees do. You may have to commit to a certain investment of time with your first employer to be taken seriously enough to receive significant responsibilities.

Currently, Baby Boomers make up nearly half of the workforce, but that's about to change as the oldest Boomers begin retiring in the next few years. Together, the two younger generations *combined* (Gen. X and Millennials) are almost as numerous as the Boomers. Nevertheless, you can expect that Boomer values will continue to dominate in the workplace for a while longer.

The key to succeeding in an intergenerational workplace is understanding where the other generations are coming from. You will have to exhibit patience and pay some dues, as older employees had to do before you. You should remain optimistic, however, for as the Baby Boomers retire, you can expect to see rapid opportunities for advancement. Resolve to learn everything you can from the older generations on your first job. You may find that older supervisors do not expect to hear much from younger employees at the lower end of the organizational hierarchy. Some older managers don't think they should have to explain things to new employees and expect them to "sink or swim." Don't be afraid to speak up when you need more explanation, but be careful not to badger your boss with constant emails or questions. This may be accepted by your friends and peers, but older managers may not appreciate it.

When you understand where employees from other generations are coming from and recognize both their contributions and hard-earned experience, you will enjoy better relationships and communication with your future coworkers. Remember that each generation has unique contributions to offer, just as you do as a much-needed younger member of the latest generation in the workforce.

The Sky's the Limit

It's definitely a great time to be a young person joining the workforce. You are entering an era of unparalleled employment opportunity and you should be engaging in blue sky thinking. While there will certainly be bumps in the road ahead, you have every reason to be optimistic and enthusiastic about your future. The demographic stars are aligning in your favor and you are facing an employment outlook far brighter than that which met previous generations. With the proper attitude, a strong work ethic, a solid education (or at least a willingness to learn), good interpersonal skills, and ambition, there is no limit to how far you can go. So put on your sunglasses and prepare to face the unlimited potential of a bright bright future. **AIM HIGH AND GOOD LUCK!**

Of course, the expected job outlook varies by field and by industry, as is detailed in the coming chapter. Keep reading to discover where the job prospects will be best. Finally, we conclude by listing hundreds of collected facts confirming the demographic changes that will be affecting the employment market and your job prospects during the coming decades.

Labor Forecasts by Industry

Labor forecasts vary depending on the specific field or industry. Certain fields that are in particularly high demand or that require skilled and technically proficient workers are going to face more critical shortages than others. In anticipation of these shortages, the U.S. Department of Labor has designated certain fields as being "High Growth." This means that the field is economically critical, projected to add substantial numbers of new jobs, and being transformed by technology and innovation. These industries include **Advanced Manufacturing, Aerospace, Automotive, Biotechnology, Construction, Energy, Financial Services, Geospatial Technology, Health Care, Homeland Security, Hospitality, Information Technology, NanoTechnology, Retail, and Transportation**. Of course, the workplace is changing so rapidly these days that entirely new careers are being created.

New "New" Careers

Many jobs that don't even exist yet will be the hot new jobs by the time this year's college freshmen graduate. Here are just a few of the hottest jobs you can get now, according to a survey by Business 2.0:

Disease Mapper

Robot Programmer

Information Engineer

Radiosurgeon

Other hot new fields include biotechnology, energy technology, epidemiology and genetic screening. We are going to need drugmakers, chemists, and researchers. The aging population means certain traditional fields will see higher demands, such as tourism, domestic support services, and financial advising. The boom in energy demand means that we will need a new generation of geologists and petroleum engineers.

The industries most likely to be affected by Baby Boomer retirements include **Educational Services, Public Administration, Transportation, and Health Services**. The 10 occupations that have been cited by the Bureau of Labor Statistics as those most likely to be affected by Boomer retirements are: **Secretaries; Heavy Truck Drivers; Elementary School Teachers; Janitors and Cleaners; Secondary School Teachers; Registered Nurses; Bookkeeping, Accounting, and Auditing Clerks; College and University Teachers; Educational and other administrators; and Farmers**. Even the government is in need of replacement workers, as almost half of the Federal Government's 1.8 million workers are at eligible retirement age.[15] This includes work ranging from homeland security to federal law enforcement to the IRS and the FDA. Now let's turn our attention to some of the specific job opportunities by field.

HEALTHCARE

The United States spends more on health care than any other nation on earth. The aging of our population will entail sharply increased needs for healthcare services of every kind, but we already have a shortage of workers in the field. The need for healthcare workers, already at dangerously high levels, will only intensify in the coming years. It is a guaranteed growth area.

Right now the biggest shortages are among registered nurses, with over 126,000 unfilled openings, nationwide. These figures are expected to worsen. According to Fitch Inc., a Wall Street Bond Rating Firm, there will be a shortfall of approximately 1 million nurses by 2010 and 1.5 million by 2020.[16] Other estimates put the number at half that, which is still a huge shortfall. Regardless of the exact numbers in the projections, we have to ask: who will take care of the largest generation of ailing elderly in the history of our country?

It's not just nurses who are in short supply, however. There are *already* shortages over 10% of imaging technicians (15.3%), licensed practical nurses (12.9%), and pharmacists (12.7%), and these shortages will only increase in the years ahead. Young people with the talent and foresight to enter the health professionals will see an enormous demand for their expertise and services in the coming labor shortages.

Aging Baby Boomers will increase their demand for healthcare services just as the pool of available healthcare workers simultaneously dwindles. Our aging population is already increasing the number of inpatient admissions and outpatient procedures, nationwide. "This makes healthcare the fastest growing and most economically sound industry sector … The massive Boomer population is overcrowding hospitals again, just the way they did when so many of them were born within a short time span. But now Boomers are aging, they require more specialized care, and their demands for care will only increase as they continue to age. More than ever, health care facilities need well-trained staff."[17]

Technology is advancing rapidly in the medical field, and the younger generations are most capable of learning and using the newest innovations. According to experts, "the youngest employees will be in much greater demand than they are today because they're needed to do the job, and they're the only ones who know how to work the technology."[18] Fields such as health care, hospitals and other organizations are confronted with vacancies as high as 50 percent. Technical advances in the field of lifesciences are increasing the need for highly skilled workers and technicians, but they are not being produced quickly enough. Already, hospital administrators are reporting significant shortages of registered nurses, radiology technicians, pharmacists, laboratory technicians and licensed practical nurses.[19] Many hospitals are having to resort to hiring expensive temporary help, to fill gaps. As expected, the demand for home health aides is also increasing tremendously.

Some hospitals and other healthcare organizations are confronted with vacancies as high as 50 percent! For example, the U.S. Department of Health and Human Services reported that nursing homes currently need 181,000 to 310,000 nurse aides to reach full staff levels.

Health care has been designated as a "High Growth Industry" by the U.S. Department of Labor, with the following "In-Demand" jobs expected to grow faster or much faster than average and to face the most severe labor shortages within the next 5-7 years:

Forecast through 2014 for Highest-Demand Jobs:

	Number of jobs	Percentage growth
Registered Nurses	3,096,100	29%
Nursing Aides, Orderlies	1,780,600	22%
Home Health Aides:	973,700	56%
Personal Care Aides	988,500	41%
Licensed Practical Nurses	850,000	17%
Medical Assistants:	586,000	52%
Medical Secretaries	436,500	17%
Health Service Managers	304,700	23%
Pharmacists/Pharmacy Techs	286,600	25%
Dental Assistants/Hygienists	271,000	43%
Physical Therapists	211,300	37%
Medical Records Personnel	204,700	29%

Medical Lab Technologists	187,800	21%
Medical Lab Technicians	183,300	25%
Rehabilitation Counselors	162,000	24%
Respiratory Therapists	120,300	28%

Source: Bureau of Labor Statistics

INFORMATION TECHNOLOGY

The field of Information Technology is also designated as a "High Growth Industry" by the Department of Labor. Skilled technicians will continue to be in high demand in the future. Many Information Technology jobs in the United States continue to remain unfilled, due to an ongoing lack of qualified applicants. The United States currently has a national IT workforce of 10.4 million, but over 450,000 vacancies went unfilled in 2001 because of the "Talent Gap"—a short-fall of workers with required skills—according to a report issued by the Information Technology Association of America (ITAA.)

The skilled labor shortage in IT has already resulted in large-scale hiring of foreign workers to overcome shortages of American skilled workers. The ITAA report goes on to point out that Information Technology employment remains at the forefront of the U.S. economy, and accounts for 7 percent of the nation's workforce. It is interesting to note that most Information Technology workers are employed by non-IT firms.

No industry in the past five years has remained significantly untouched by technology and the pace of advance is accelerating. Businesses will continue to need savvy staff to help them navigate the technology, and those businesses will continue to pay their young experts well because they are scarce.

This is definitely a field in which young people have the upper hand. One of the ironies of modern times is that with the advent of technology, young workers may actually be more "experienced" than their bosses. The traditional employee model has always envisioned younger workers learning, apprenticeship style, from older employees. Only after a number of years of soaking up information would the younger worker be considered to have the knowledge necessary for higher levels of responsibility.

The internet and the computer changed all that. Because older generations have had a harder time getting "up to speed" with newer technologies, for the first time ever, it is the youngest workers who control knowledge access to one of the most important and fundamental elements of daily business life. If a computer virus strikes or the server goes down and the system needs rebooting, it is the young employee who is most likely to be the one called upon to handle the job. Information technology "is the rare field where a tattooed, pierced, orange-haired kid [can] hold his conservative-suited Boomer … boss in the palm of his hand because this kid is the only one who knows what is going on inside the server. What does that mean? It means good pay and a pretty solid future"[20]

According to generational consultant Cam Marston, "When young, technologically adept employees enter a workplace that is largely staffed by senior employees who are confused by and fearful of technology, a genuine role reversal takes place—quite a rare occurrence in our civilized world. Youth is the master, bypassing the apprentice stage altogether."[21] Marston argues that "the introduction of technology to business operations immediately changed the dues-paying process in this one arena … For the first time in history the younger generation of employees controlled a critical aspect of business."[22] In this respect, knowledge of technology equates with earning power in the workforce.

Forecast through 2014 for Highest-Demand Jobs:

	Number of jobs	Percentage growth
Software Engineers/Applications	682,2000	48%
Computer Systems Analysts	639,500	31%
Computer Support Specialists	637,600	23%
Software Engineers/Software – Systems	486,500	43%
Network Systems Analysts	357,500	55%
Computer systems administrators	385,200	38%
Computer Programmers	464,300	2%
Database Administrators	144,300	38%

Source: Bureau of Labor Statistics

EDUCATION AND SOCIAL SERVICES

One field that is going to experience a particularly serious demographic turnover is Education, both K-12 and postsecondary. Schools and colleges nationwide will soon face a mass exodus of the majority of their workforce, as tenured Baby Boomers retire. According to the National Education Association, **more than a million veteran teachers are nearing retirement, and we will need more than two million new teachers in the next decade**.

Beyond the retirement problem, the statistics for turnover among new teachers are shocking: nearly 50 percent of teachers leave the profession within five years. Two-thirds of the nation's mathematics and science teaching force will retire by 2010. Forty percent of the current public school teaching force does not plan to be teaching five years from now, and the K-12 teaching force is aging rapidly. The proportion of K-12 teachers who are 50 years of age and older has risen from one in four (24%) in 1996 to 42% in 2005. Nearly three quarters of a million K-12 teachers will retire by 2010. That is nearly 30% of the entire teaching force! Likewise, Social Service agencies will have plentiful vacancies for qualified applicants during the coming labor shortage.

Forecast through 2014 for Highest-Demand Jobs:

	Number of jobs	Percentage growth
Postsecondary teachers	2,152,600	32%
Elementary school teachers	1,922,200	18%
Secondary school teachers	1,172,200	14%
Teacher assistants	1,478,200	14%
Middle school teachers	714,100	14%
Special education teachers (K-12)	534,100	23%
Mental health counselor	269,000	27%
School administrators (K-12)	249,000	10%

Community Service Manager	168,500	26%
College administrators	159,800	21%
Preschool/childcare administrators	74,700	28%

Source: Bureau of Labor Statistics

MANAGEMENT

The management ranks of American businesses are already stretched very thin, and leaner organizations have been trying to get more done with fewer people for decades now. This situation is likely to continue and the demand for management workers is expected to grow faster than average during the coming decade. Highly qualified graduates with leadership and management potential can expect rapid advancement opportunities during the coming labor shortage.

We may even soon see a return to the days of signing bonuses and other premium hiring incentives, as well as competition between headhunters and top firms doing whatever they can to lure top talent.

Forecast through 2014 for Highest-Demand Jobs:

	Number of jobs	Percentage growth
Financial Managers	606,300	15%
Training and Development Specialists	260,800	21%
First-line supervisors/Personal service	243,700	18%
Employment/Recruitment Specialists	237,400	30%
Marketing Managers	227,700	21%
Human Resources Assistant	200,200	17%
Compensation/Benefits Managers	188,800	21%
Public Relations Manager	70,000	22%
Training and development managers	47,000	26%

Source: Bureau of Labor Statistics

BUSINESS AND RETAIL

Competition for qualified retail workers will intensify in the coming labor short-age, as will efforts to reduce turnover by improving retention statistics. The demand for employees in business and financial operations will remain strong, with particularly high demand expected for accountants, computer support, and personal financial planners. As Baby Boomers age, they will need assistance with managing their finances, so demand for personal financial advisors is expected to increase. The fields expected to grow faster than average include:

Forecast through 2014 for Highest-Demand Jobs:

	Number of jobs	Percentage growth
Retail Salespersons	4,991,900	17%
Customer Service Representatives	2,534,200	23%
Executive secretary/admin. assistant	1,739,300	12%
Accountants and Auditors	1,440,100	22%
Sales Representatives	569,000	14%
Billing Agents	540,800	3%
Sales Managers	402,700	20%
Marketing Managers	227,700	21%
Personal Financial Advisors	199,000	26%
Compensation/Benefits Manager	69,800	21%

Source: Bureau of Labor Statistics

SALES

Talented sales professionals are always in demand. The top sellers can command very high incomes, indeed. As Thomas Watson, the founder of IBM, wisely pointed out, "Nothing happens until somebody sells something." Likewise, managing customer relations throughout the selling process is essential to sales completion and fulfillment, and customer services representatives are going to be in particularly high demand during the coming years. Across the board, expect to see steady, consistent growth in demand for sales professionals during the coming years.

Forecast through 2014 for Highest-Demand Jobs:

	Number of jobs	Percentage growth
Customer service representatives	2,534,200	23%
Sales representatives, non-technical	1,641,100	13%
Customer support specialists	637,600	23%
Driver/sales workers	513,400	14%
Sales representatives, technical	454,500	14%
Sales managers	402,000	20%
Securities sales agents	313,000	12%
Advertising sales agents	179,600	16%
Demonstrators and product promoters	137,500	16%

Source: Bureau of Labor Statistics

MANUFACTURING

Much has already been written about the decline of the American manufacturing sector, and the coming labor shortage will only exacerbate the situation. With cheap labor to be found overseas, outsourcing is being touted as the solution to America's limited labor pool and competitive advantage. However, loss of manufacturing potential places America in a potential strategic and economic disadvantage. Nevertheless, anticipated job growth will be continue to be very high among engineering departments of industrial manufacturing firms.

Forecast through 2014 for Highest-Demand Jobs:

	Number of jobs	Percentage growth
Supervisors-Production workers	750,300	3%
Helpers-Production workers	521,800	8%
Production and expediting clerks	314,500	8%
Mechanical engineers	251,000	11%
Industrial engineers	205,000	16%
Electrical engineers	174,300	12%
Industrial production managers	161,600	1%
Industrial engineering technicians	76,000	10%
Chemical engineers	33,900	11%

Source: Bureau of Labor Statistics

Where the Job Opportunities Are Best

Top 25 Occupations with the Most Openings through 2014
Requirement: On-the-Job Training

Retail Salesperson

Cashiers

Waiters and waitresses

Food preparation and servers, including fast food

Freight, stock and material movers

Office clerks

Janitors and cleaners

Customer Service representatives

Stock clerks and order fillers

Sales representatives (non-technical)

Child care workers

Receptionists and information clerks

Truck drivers

Executive secretaries and administrative assistants

Landscaping and groundskeeping workers

Maids and housekeeping workers

Maintenance and repair workers

First-line supervisors of office workers

Teacher assistants

Home health aides

Team assemblers

Carpenters

Personal and home care aides
Counter attendants (food service)
Cooks, restaurant

Source: Bureau of Labor Statistics

Top 25 Occupations with the Most Openings through 2014
Requirement: Postsecondary Training

Registered nurses

Nursing aides, orderlies, and attendants

Automotive service technicians and mechanics

Licensed practical nurses

Hairdressers and cosmetologists

Preschool teachers

Computer support specialists

Medical secretaries

Real estate sales agents

Bus and truck mechanics

Fitness trainers

Legal secretaries

Paralegals and legal assistants

Dental hygienists

Medical and clinical laboratory technicians

Radiologic technologists

EMT/paramedic

Medical records and health information technicians

Library technicians

Respiratory therapists

Electrical engineering technicians

Gaming dealers

Appraisers and assessors of real estate

Aircraft mechanics and service technicians

Medical transcriptionists

Source: Bureau of Labor Statistics

Top 25 Occupations with the Most Openings through 2014
Requirement: Bachelor's degree or above

Postsecondary teachers

General and operations managers

Elementary school teachers

Accountants and auditors

Secondary school teachers

Computer software engineers

Middle school teachers

Physicians and surgeons

Computer systems analysts

Lawyers

Management analysts

Computer software engineers

Financial managers

Network systems and data communications analysts

Chief executives

Clergy

Network and computer systems administrators

Sales managers

Computer and information systems managers

Property, real estate, and community association managers

Construction managers

Insurance sales agents

Computer programmers

Medical and health services managers

Pharmacists

Source: Bureau of Labor Statistics

Further Career Information

A successful career search begins with knowing where to gather reliable information. The following websites are useful resources to begin your career search:

http://www.acinet.org/acinet/

http://www.bls.gov/oco

http://www.careeronestop.org/

http://online.onetcenter.org/

These websites can provide you with accurate information about the requirements for different careers, salary information, and much more.

Also, be sure to notify your friends and family that you are looking for a job; they may hear of opportunities that would be of interest to you. It is also important to check with your school's career counseling center. Recruiters often come to campuses looking for applicants, and it is helpful to sign up early for interviewing slots.

The Facts

Starting in 2012, nearly 10,000 Americans will turn 65 every day. 20% of the population, 71 million people, will be 65 or older in 2030. The total number of Americans over age 65 and eligible for Medicare will double to over 70 million within this generation, while the population over age 85 will increase nearly five-fold, to almost 19 million, by mid-century.

—Source: Social Security Administration

Between 1870 and 1990, the number of U.S. citizens aged 65 and older grew from 1 million to approximately 32 million. By 2030, the proportion of people over 65 will be 20% of the population.

—Source: U.S. Census

The labor force of 16-to 19-year-olds was 7.8 million in 1990, 8.3 million in 2000, and 7.2 million in 2005; it is projected to decrease until 2020 and then gradually increase, reaching 7.2 million again in 2050.

—Source: Monthly Labor Review

By 2012, nearly 20% of the total U.S. workforce will be 55 or older, up from just under 13% in 2000.

—Source: "Labor Force Projections to 2012:
The Graying of the U.S. Workforce," Monthly Labor Review, February 2004

The number of workers age 55 and over is growing four times faster than the workforce as a whole. Baby boomers, who in 2006 ranged in age from 42 to 60, currently represent one-half of the U.S. workforce. This is slightly more than the combined number of workers from the succeeding two generations, Generation X and Millennial Generation (Generation Y).

—Source: The Aging of the U.S. Workforce: Employer Challenges and Responses,
January 2006, Ernst & Young

Between 2000 and 2010, the number of U.S. workers ages 45-54 is projected to grow by just over 20%, while the number of those ages 55-64 is projected to grow more than 50%. In contrast, the number of workers ages 35-44 is projected to decrease by 10%.

—Source: The Aging of the U.S. Workforce: Employer Challenges and Responses, January 2006, Ernst & Young

The percentage of people 55-64 will increase by more than 50 percent between 2000 and 2010, while the number of people 35-44 will decline by more than 10 percent.

—Source: Atlanta Business Chronicle

Today out of a total population of nearly 300 million, approximately 35.9 million people are age 65 or older, or about 1 of every 8 Americans. By the year 2030, people age 65 and older are projected to make up 24% of the population, nearly 1 of every 4 Americans.

—Source: The Aging of the U.S. Workforce: Employer Challenges and Responses, January 2006, Ernst & Young

The labor force participation rate of 16-to 19-year-olds was 53.7 percent in 1990, declined to 52.0 percent in 2000, and fell further to 43.7 percent in 2005. The Bureau projects that the downward trend in the participation rate of 16-to 19-year-olds will continue and the rate will reach 34.5 percent in 2050. This is mainly due to increased rates of school attendance.

—Source: Monthly Labor Review

According to the U.S. Bureau of Labor Statistics, more than 25% of the working population will reach retirement age by 2010, resulting in a potential worker shortage of nearly 10 million.

According to the U.S. Census Bureau, the number of people aged 55 and older will increase by 73% by 2020, while the number of younger workers will grow only 5%.

There are now more people over 90 or 100 than in all of American history put together.

In 1950, there were 7 working age people for every elderly person in the United States. By 2030, there will be only 3.

Since 1950, the number of people aged 65 and older in the United States has increased from 8% to 12%.

By 2008, the number of young adult workers, from 25-to 40-year-olds, will DECLINE by 1.7 million. That's 1.7 million fewer workers to replace the nearly 77 million baby boomers who will be eligible for retirement.

The 50 and older population from 2000-2050 will grow at a rate 68 times faster than the rate of growth for the total population.

—*Source: Beyond Workforce 2020, Hudson Institute*

By the middle of this century, there will be more older people than children on the planet for the first time in human history.

—*Source: AARP Global Aging Program*

The labor force participation rate of 20-to 24-year-olds was 77.8 percent in both 1990 and 2000. In 2005, the rate declined significantly, to 74.6 percent. The participation rate of the 20-to 24-year age group is projected to decrease further, to 73.8 percent in 2020 and 73.1 percent in 2050. The decrease in the labor force participation rate of youths—especially 16-to 19-year-old men—has been a major contributor to the decrease in the overall labor force participation rate.

—*Source: Monthly Labor Review*

As of 2004, there were 73.4 million people younger than 18 in the U.S., or approximately 25% of the population. In 1970, the percentage of the population under 18 was 34%. By 2010, the number will be only 24%.

—*Source: childstats.gov*

In 1990, there were 37,306 Americans who were at least 100 years old. By the year 2010, there will be 131,000. And, by 2050, projections by the U.S. Census Bureau anticipate there being 834,000 centenarians. To put that figure in perspective, those 834,000 people who will be at least 100 years old in 2050 would outnumber the current populations of cities such as Baltimore, Indianapolis, San Francisco, Boston, or Denver. In fact, they would surpass the populations of all but the top 11 U.S. cities counted in the 2000 Census.

The share of the labor force aged 55 and older is rising rapidly. By 2020, the share of the labor force held by those 55 years and older is projected to be nearly 24 percent.

—Source: Monthly Labor Review

The workplace makeup has changed dramatically from just a decade ago. In 1996 there were 64 million U.S. workers between the ages of 30 and 39 and only 43 million ages 40 to 59.

Now the situation has reversed. As of June 2006 there were only 40 million ages 30 to 39 and 69 million workers 40 to 59.

—Source: Bureau of Labor Statistics

Up to now, the number of senior citizens has been steadily creeping higher, but the number of workers has been roughly keeping pace. This will change in 2008, when the first group of boomers, born in 1946, reaches age 62—the age at which most people begin collecting Social Security benefits. Soon after, they will qualify for Medicare. At this point, the number of new workers entering the workforce will begin to decline.

—Source: Social Security Administration

In 2002, 12.4% of the U.S. population was 65 and older. Over the next 30 years, this proportion will rise to 20%.

—Source: Bureau of Labor Statistics

There are 39.4 million people in the 26-35 age group versus 44.2 million in the 36-45 age group.

—Source: Employment Policy Foundation

The aging population is a global phenomenon. Other countries with similar predicaments include Russia, Germany, the UK, Japan, France and Spain.

—Source: Employment Policy Foundation

Over 50% of boomers lived in the following nine states (in 2000): California, Texas, New York, Florida, Pennsylvania, Illinois, Ohio, Michigan and New Jersey.

—Source: MetLife Mature Market Institute

By the end of this decade, there will be a 12 percent decline in the 35 to 44-age segment and a 3 percent decline in the 30 to 34 age group. Unless there is another big jump in immigration, by 2010 there will be at least 5 million fewer workers ages 30 to 44 than there are now.

—Source: Census Bureau

The number of U.S. workers between ages 55 and 64 will grow 51% to 25 million by 2012, meaning the fastest-growing portion of the workforce is the one at most risk of retiring soon. At the same time, the number of workers between ages 35 and 44 is expected to shrink by 7%.

—Source: Wall Street Journal, Sept. 20, 2005

The annual growth rate of the U.S. population ages 15-64, the traditional working age population, is projected at 0.3%. The comparable rate for ages 65 and over is projected at 3.1%. Almost 90% of the net increase in the traditional working age population is projected to occur in the age 55-64 group.

—Source: The Aging of the U.S. Workforce: Employer Challenges and Responses, January 2006, Ernst & Young

Although 41 million people are expected to enter the American workforce by 2010, 46 million college-educated baby boomers will retire in the next 20 years. More than 40% of the U.S. labor force will reach traditional retirement age by the end of the decade. At the same time, the number of workers between ages 35 and 44 is expected to shrink by 7%.

—Source: Bureau of Labor Statistics

Under current census projections, the number of working-age Americans (ages 18 to 64) to each resident 65 years and up will fall from 4.8 in the year 2000 to 2.7 in 2050.

—Source: Social Security: A Tale of Two Problems, Washington Policy Center

Americans are living longer and having fewer children, and this alters the ratio between the number of workers and retirees. In 1937, there were 42 workers to support every retiree. In 1950, there were 16 workers for each retiree. Today, there are approximately 3.3 workers for each retiree. By 2025, there will be two workers per retiree and by 2050, 1.3 workers per retiree.

—*Source: Social Security: A Tale of Two Problems, Washington Policy Center*

By 2010 we will have 167,754,000 skilled jobs to fill in the United States alone. By 2010 we will have only 157,721,000 people in the workforce to fill those jobs. Assuming that 5% of the workforce holds two jobs, we still will have approximately 2.2 million jobs unfilled.

—*Source: Human Trend Alerts, October 2002*

One-fifth of this country's large, established companies will be losing 40% or more of their top-level talent in the next five years.

—*Source: Development Dimensions International*

As 38 million baby boomers reached employment age in the 1970s and 1980s, the workplace exploded by 50%. In the decade following 2010, the portion of the population under age 45—the principal talent pool for managers and workers—will shrink by 6%.

—*Source: The Kiplinger Letter, May 17, 2002*

The demand for labor in the next decade may outpace supply by 35 million jobs:

- In 1950, 60% of all manufacturing jobs required unskilled labor.

- By 2005, less than 15% of all manufacturing positions will be unskilled.

- In 1973, blue-collar workers represented over 60% of the workforce.

- By 2000, only 10% of the workforce was blue-collar workers.

—*Source: Employment Policy Foundation*

65% of all American employment now requires specific skills.

—*Source: Bureau of Labor Statistics*

There are currently over one million unfilled jobs in Germany and Britain.

—Manpower

Nearly half the population can barely read. Only 13 percent of this country's adults have English reading and comprehension skills considered to be "proficient." Another 29 percent have just the basic skills to complete everyday tasks, as long as the reading is short and the complexity is simple. Far too many workers cannot read and understand a newspaper article written at an eighth grade reading level or complete the type of math problem that is taught in the fourth grade.

—Source: National Assessment of Adult Literacy (NAAL) study

More literacy facts:

- More than 20 percent of adults read at or below the fifth grade level.

- Forty-four million American adults are poor readers or "functionally illiterate."

- Twenty-one million American adults can't read at all; one-fifth of high school graduates can't read their diplomas.

- One-third of high school graduates never read another book for the rest of their lives.

- Forty-two percent of college graduates never read another book.

- Seventy percent of Americans haven't visited a bookstore in five or more years.

* One of the largest and fastest growing groups of young people in the U.S. is dropouts. In the United States the annual high school dropout rate hovers at 34 percent.

—Source: The Literacy Company and Evelyn Wood Reading Dynamics

Thirty years ago, the U.S. had 30 % of the world's college-educated population. Today that number is 14%.

For every 100 ninth graders:

68 graduate from high school in four years.
40 enroll directly in college after graduation

27 are still enrolled in college one year after entering

18 earned an associate degree within three years or a bachelor's degree with six years

82 don't receive a college degree

—*Source: National Center on Education and the Economy, "Tough choices or Tough Times," 2007*

According to the U.S. Census Bureau, one of the largest and fastest-growing groups of young people in the United States are dropouts, rising to almost 1 out of 3 Americans in their mid-20s.

—*Source: Organization for Economic Co-operation and Development*

The number of women obtaining degrees is outpacing that of men. Women obtained between 40% and 60% of the bachelor's degrees in mathematics and sciences in 2000.

Four-year college grads make roughly $20,000 more than their high school trained counterparts. People with two-year degrees make only about $7,000 more a year than high school grads. The bottom line: A four-year degree is becoming America's most reliable elevator of class and key to a middle-class standard of living.

—*Source: Business Week, October 31, 2005*

Within the next 10 years, 18 million jobs will require individuals with baccalaureate degrees. At the current level of graduations, we will have a shortfall of 6 million.

—*Source: Employment Policy Foundation*

In 2002, almost 35% of high school graduates in the U.S. did not go on to attend a four-year institution or a two-year college program. That's 972,000 high school grads. By 2020 we're going to have a shortfall of some 14 million skilled workers who will need some type of post-secondary education or training to qualify for the high skilled jobs our economy demands. In fact, 80% of the U.S.'s fastest-growing jobs over the next decade will require at least two years of college.

The number of women obtaining degrees is outpacing that of men. Women obtained between 40% and 60% of the bachelor's degrees in mathematics and sciences in 2000.

—Source: Time, October 24, 2005

Individuals with less than a ninth-grade education earn an estimated $976,350 over their lifetime. A high school dropout earns $1,150,968. A high school graduate earns $1,455,253. And a person with a bachelor's degree earns $2,567,174.

—Source: Federal Reserve Bank of Dallas

One out of every four agricultural jobs is held by an illegal immigrant; 17% of all office and housecleaning positions, 14% of construction jobs, and 12% of food preparation jobs also are held by undocumented workers.

—Source: Pew Hispanic Center, 2006

The number of U.S. Catholic sisters (nuns) has decreased from 180,000 in 1965 to 68,600 in 2005. The worst is yet to come—the majority is older than 70 and the younger generation shows little interest.

—Source: Center for Applied Research in the Apostolate, Georgetown University

Half of America's scientists and engineers are 40 or older, and the average age is steadily rising.

—Source: National Science Foundation

Nearly 40% of NASA employees are age 50 or older.

—Source: NASA

22% of NASA workers are 55 or older. Scientists and engineers who are over 60 at the National Aeronautics and Space Administration outnumber those under 30 by nearly 3 to 1. Only 4% of NASA workers are under 30.

—Source: NASA

According to the U.S. Bureau of Labor Statistics (BLS), more than 20% of the nation's 3.2 million federal employees were ages 55 or older in 2004. Within the next five years, *half* of the federal government's civilian workforce will be eligible for retirement.

—*Source: The Aging of the U.S. Workforce: Employer Challenges and Responses, January 2006, Ernst & Young*

Nearly 20% of 16.7 million state and local government employees were age 55 or older in 2004. In comparison, just over 14% of private sector workers were ages 55 or older in 2004.

—Source: The Aging of the U.S. Workforce: Employer Challenges and Responses, January 2006, Ernst & Young

Half of current federal employees will be eligible to retire between now and the end of 2008, including 70% of supervisors.

Half of the federal air traffic controllers are eligible to retire over the next nine years.

43% of the 650,000 civilians at the Department of Defense will be eligible in the next five years.

60% of federal employees are over 45, compared with 31% in the private sector.

—*Source: Bernard Hodes Group, Feb 2005*

The U.S. Department of Defense needs to hire more than 14,000 scientists and engineers in each of the next two years. The problem is that the pool of candidates is shrinking.

- More than half of science and engineering graduates from American universities are foreign nationals, off-limits to federal agencies

- Fewer American students are entering science and tech fields

- DOD must compete with the private sector and other government agencies.

The Census Bureau estimates that the overall pool who would be in the military's prime target age has shrunk as Americans age. There were 1 million fewer 18-to 24-year-olds in 2004 than in 2000.

Out of 32 million Americans age 17 to 24, most do not qualify to serve in the military. 2.3 million qualify for medical or misdemeanor waivers, 2.6 million disqualify due to medical problems, and 4.6 million are disqualified for criminal history, obesity, and dependents.

—Source: U.S. Army

Two-thirds of the nation's mathematics and science teaching force will retire by 2010.

—Source: National Commission on Mathematics and Science Teaching for the 21st Century

40% of the current public school teaching force expects not to be teaching five years from now.

—Source: Profile of Teachers in the U.S. 2005

The K-12 teaching force is aging rapidly. The proportion of K-12 teachers who are 50 years of age and older has risen from one in four (24%) in 1996 to 42% in 2005.

—Source: Profile of Teachers in the U.S. 2005

Teacher attrition is expected to average about 8% per year in the next five years.

—Source: Profile of Teachers in the U.S. 2005

Only 36% of doctorate-level faculty in the U.S. are currently under 45 years of age.

—Source: Time, October 24, 2005

Half (50%) of current high school teachers expect not to be teaching in K-12 schools in 2010. One-third (34%) of high school teachers plan to be retired by then.

—Source: Profile of Teachers in the U.S. 2005

By 2010, nearly 30%, or 765,000, of our nation's public school teachers will retire.

—Source: U.S. Dept. of Education

Nearly 75% of U.S. hospital emergency departments report a shortage of specialists such as neurosurgeons and orthopedists.

—Source: American College of Emergency Physicians, 2006

The demand for intensive care physicians will continue to exceed available supply through the year 2020 if current supply and demand trends continue.

—Source: Department of Health and Human Services Administration Report, 2006

The U.S. had a shortage of 1,200 critical care doctors in 2000. The HRSA report projected the shortage will rise to 1,500 in 2020.

—Source: Department of Health and Human Services Administration Report, 2006

Between 1950 and 1999 the number of people in the labor force grew from 62.2 million to 139.4 million, an increase of 77.2 million. Of that number, women were 46.5 million or 60 percent.

—Source: Labor Force by Sex and Age, 1950 to 2025

The proportion of bachelor's degrees awarded to women reached a post-war high in 2003 at an estimated 57%.

—Source: Employment Policy Foundation

By 2030, women will hold a larger share of management and professional jobs than men.

—Source: Employment Policy Foundation

The labor participation rate of men has been continually decreasing, having registered 76.4 percent in 1990, 74.8 percent in 2000, and 73.3 percent in 2005. The rate is projected to be 70.0 percent in 2020 and 66.0 percent in 2050.

—Source: Monthly Labor Review

The aging of the health workforce raises concerns that many health professionals will retire about the same time that demand for their services is increasing. Furthermore, the declining proportion of the population age 18 to 30 raises concerns regarding the ability to attract a sufficient number of new health workers.

—Source: HRSA

The aging population will increase the demand for physicians per thousand population from 2.8 in 2000 to 3.1 in 2020. Demand for full-time-equivalent (FTE) registered nurses per thousand population would increase from 7 to 7.5 during this same period.

—Source: HRSA

The aging population could result in rising average patient acuity, which could in turn require higher nurse and physician staffing levels.

—Source: HRSA

Endnotes

1. Ranstad work solutions. *The World of Work 2007*. Harris Interactive: p. 26

2. Ranstad, p. 26.

3. Eisenberg, D. (April 29, 2002.) "The Coming Job Boom." *Time* Magazine.

4. Kotlikoff, L. and Burns, S. (2005.) *The Coming Generational Storm: What You Need to Know About America's Economic Future*, MIT: Cambridge.

5. National Center on Education and the Economy, p. 8.

6. National Center, p. 5.

7. National Center, p. 6.

8. National Center, p. 6.

9. National Center, pp. 8,9.

10. The Conference Board, p. 7.

11. The Conference Board, p. 36.

12. The Conference Board, pp. 36-38.

13. Adapted from The Conference Board, p. 41.

14. National Center, p. 9.

15. Eisenberg, D. (April 29, 2002.) "The Coming Job Boom." *Time* Magazine.

16. Herman, R., Olivo, T., and Gioia, J. (2003.) *Impending Crisis: Too Many Jobs, Too Few People*. Oakhill Press: VA.

17. Marston, C. (2007.) *Motivating the "What's In It For Me" Workforce: Manage Across the Generational Divide and Increase Profits*. USA: Wiley, p. 177.

18. Marston, p. 178.

19. Deloitte & Touche: *The Future of Health Care: An Outlook from the Perspective of Hospital CEOs.*

20. Marston, pp. 179, 180.

21. Marston, p. 6.

22. Marston, p. 68.

About the Authors

Intuitive, practical, and down-to-earth is the way Dr. Ira Wolfe has been described by clients and colleagues. As founder of Success Performance Solutions and president of Poised for the Future Company, his approach to employee selection and performance management has earned him the endorsement and respect of both business leaders as well as consultants. While helping a client to build a national sales force, Ira designed a blueprint for selection, hiring, development, and succession planning, which became CriteriaOne®: The Whole Person Approach, used by dozens of consultants, small businesses, and Fortune 500 companies.

Ira might be best known for the "Perfect Labor Storm" term he coined in 1999, describing events leading up to the largest shortage of skilled workers in American history. Since then he has been speaking and publishing two newsletters: the monthly *Labor Storm Alert* and the weekly *The Total View*.

His audiences have included the National Association of Home Builders, Institute of Management Consultants, Society of Human Resource Management, and the American Society of Training and Development.

Dr. Bonnie Kerrigan Snyder is a higher education professional and writer with particular interests in career and education issues. A former college career counselor and certified guidance counselor, Dr. Snyder has taught graduate level courses in Career Development and continues to teach at the college level. A professional copywriter, she has worked for numerous corporate clients in the United States and abroad. She has also been published in newspapers and magazines, and she is the author of The *Public School Parent's Guide to Success: How to Beat Private School and Homeschooling*, available at www.publicschoolparent.com.

Contact the Authors

For information about career testing to identify your perfect career and career strengths, contact Dr. Wolfe through:

Websites: www.super-solutions.com or www.comingjobboom.com

Email: iwolfe@super-solutions.com or iwolfe@perfectlaborstorm.com

Phone: 1.800.803.4303

You can reach Dr. Snyder through:

Websites: www.bonnieksnyder.com or www.comingjobboom.com

Email: bonnie@bonnieksnyder.com

Give the gift of a bright future!

To order additional copies of *The Coming JOB BOOM*,
Visit www.comingjobboom.com

References

The Conference Board, Partnership for 21st Century Skills, Corporate Voices for Working Families, and Society for Human Resource Management. (2006.) *Are They Really Ready to Work? Employers' Perspectives on the Basic Knowledge and Applied Skills of New Entrants to the 21st Century U.S. Workforce.* USA.

Deloitte & Touche: *The Future of Health Care: An Outlook from the Perspective of Hospital CEOs.*

Herman, R. Olivo, T. Gioia, J. (2003.) *Impending Crisis: Too Many Jobs, Too Few People.* USA: Oakhill Press.

Kotlikoff, L. and Burns, S. (2005.) *The Coming Generational Storm: What You Need to Know about America's Economic Future.* Cambridge: MIT Press.

Marston, C. (2007.) *Motivating the "What's In It For Me" Workforce: Manage Across the Generational Divide and Increase Profits.* USA: Wiley.

Martin, C. And Tulgan, B. (2002.) *Managing the Generation Mix: From Collision to Collaboration.* Amherst, MA: HRD Press.

National Center on Education and the Economy. (2007.) *Tough Choices or Tough Times: The Report of the New Commission on the Skills of the American Workforce.* Jossey-Bass: USA.

Ranstad work solutions. (2007.) *The World of Work 2007.* Harris Interactive:

Ten Questions to Consider Before Accepting a Job Offer

1. How will this organization utilize the skills that I have?

2. What kind of training or coaching opportunities does the organization provide for current employees?

3. What responsibilities will I have?

4. What kinds of goals will I need to meet?

5. What will I be doing on a day-to-day basis?

6. How often will I receive feedback from my manager?

7. How often will my performance be evaluated?

8. Who will I be working with? Will I have an opportunity to meet them?

9. What opportunities exist for me to accept more responsibilities, move laterally or move up in the organization?

10. Can you give me an example of a current employee who had similar experience and expertise to me who was promoted? How long did it take him/her?

How Will YOU Choose YOUR Next Employer?

In less than 15 minutes you can complete a short online questionnaire which will provide you with a description of the best job environment and culture for your personality and skills as well as *interview questions you should be asking* your next employer.

This $47 value is available at the special price of $20 for readers of this book. To learn more about our Online Career Tests, go to:

www.comingjobboom.com/jobclues

Find the Right Job for YOU!

Confused about choosing a career? Unhappy in your current position and unsure if you are on the right career path? Contact us about our World of Work Inventory (WOWI). WOWI is designed to measure an individual's uniqueness related to specific job tasks, worker trait characteristics, and desired life style.

To learn more about WOWI and receive a 50% off coupon, visit:

www.comingjobboom.com/jobclues

978-0-595-48316-7
0-595-48316-X